The Snow Birds

by Zoë Clarke

illustrated by Ciara Ni Dhuinn

Winter had come. Thick snow lay on the ground. It glinted like glass.

Rav was staying with his grandad. Now they were snowed in!

“Right!” said Grandad. “Let’s get the brushes out.”

First, they swept each step.

“Next, we will clear the path,” said Grandad.

Rav enjoyed clearing the snow away.

"Can we go to the woods now?" Rav asked.

"Yes!" said Grandad.

They crunched down the track.

“Look!” said Grandad, pointing. “The stream has swirling patterns.”

They saw footprints in the snow. The wood was still.

Rav shivered.

"I miss the summer birds," he sighed.

In bed that night, Rav dreamed about birds.

Rav looked down from his window the following morning.

"Snow birds!" he gasped.

“Well, well,” said Grandad.

Rav pulled on his boots. He ran into the garden.

“This one has wings like an owl. This one has spots like a thrush,” Rav said.

"Have they come from the wood?" Rav asked.

"They have come from the snow," Grandad replied.

The next day, there were flocks of snow birds!

Rav found a clue.

“Grandad! You did this,” he said.

Grandad showed Rav how he modelled the snow birds.

Then they modelled snow cats and dogs. They twisted twigs into crowns. They added dried flowers.

That night, the gardens were lit up with torches. The snow animals looked like living things.

Rav sat with Grandad in the garden.

"I like your snow birds best," Rav said.

Winter did not last. Soon the snow birds melted. Just the twigs and dried flowers were left.

Rav stayed with Grandad in the spring. They squelched into the woods.

Lots of birds were nesting in the trees.

"Look!" Grandad said. "The stream is swirling with water."

"I love the spring," Rav said. "Then in winter, we can enjoy the snow birds."

Look Back

Encourage students to use the map to retell the story. Where were the snow birds found?